'WHISPERINGS' May 2018

Health

A medical doctor of many years recently gave his advice on health to people. He said the best thing people can do for their health is to avoid hospitals, drugs, and eat vegetables. Hospitals are full of disease, infections, and health problems. Many, if not most drugs, just treat the symptoms and are not a cure.

Since the human body is 70% water, it makes all kinds of sense to hydrate your body. If water is lacking, the cells cannot function properly. Waste builds up and toxicity develops. All this is well and good, but there is even a more alarming component of health from relationships.

The most important discovery of a person's life regarding health is a personal relationship with the Creator of the soul and body. His Presence is health itself. Absence His Presence is disease and sickness. There is Presence in Name only and there is

Presence as in a Temple, which by the way, the Creator says just such a thing about the human body. It is His Temple.

Then there is the presence of another person in conversation communication. What is important is not the subject matter of the conversation, but the connecting presence. It is the company, not the brilliant conversation which matters little regarding health. Oh, there may sometimes be good advice, but the main purpose of friends is simply bonding, sharing the moments, being together. Yes, advice may be timely but is often uninvited. Fellowship, friendship, the presence of another is healthy. Without it, there is ultimately sickness. Some people can live alone, but they are few. Even they need to be in the company of people.

Trans

This adjective means across from one side to another. When it relates to sex birth and identity it is used as an adjective, like trans male meaning born male but with personal identity as female. People are becoming more open today and identifying themselves in a large range of identities from male to female and vise-versa.

People are born this way because their parents and grandparents have had dysfunctional relationships with the Divine. Their children now experience the results. Romans chapter one explains that this happens when people do not give respect and thanks to the Creator whose Deity is clearly seen by the glory of Creation. So the Divine gives people like this over to darkened minds and sinful desires of their hearts.

Relationships with the Divine are oriented in the heart of people. It is not just going to Church, or even being born again, though this is a step in the right direction. The Lord looks upon the heart of a person where relationships are formed. Remember the Divine sought out David, the son of Jesse, to replace King Saul because David's heart was strongly oriented to the Divine.

Honesty is a good thing. All this coming out will just help clear the air so humans can begin to deal better with where we are. Keeping it hidden is not a solution. The cure, so to speak, is a relationship issue with the Divine, not a matter of choice of sex identity. Blaming people for their sex identity is futile as they are born this way from generations of parents whose distant ignoring relationship with the Holy is the cause. This digital age is flooding the world with information and bringing people together faster than they can deal with it. If people have relatives who are trans this n' that it is better to accept them in their struggle to deal with their self-image and identity crisis. Usually those who blame others are more of the problem than the cure. Fault finding is only the first step in the right direction. Cure developments are the next steps if we want to make progress.

Closeness

To be alone without close friends and ultimately the One who matters the most, is an awful feeling. People have many acquaintances, but few friends and even fewer close ones. This is so because it takes time to experience friends. There are only so many hours in the day. Things need to be done. Besides sleep, there is work, cleaning, repair, immediate family, doctors, illness, and then the remaining hours become very valuable. The older people become, the more precious the hours and in some cases minutes. In the midst of all this activity a sense of loneliness can creep into a person's life. This is a signal that the Best Friend is waiting to draw closer.

"One who has unreliable friends soon comes to ruin, but there is a friend who sticks closer than a brother." Proverbs 18:24

Food and stomach, air and lungs, education and brain are all made for each other and will perish in time with the using. Now we come to the soul of man. It was made for the Divine and the Divine for the soul. Neither will perish in time with the search for closeness. It is the greatest feeling in the world and beyond when the Divine has our

back every day. This is the meaning of life
and how it plays out daily is the design of
each person's gift. This close relationship
operates through faith, hope and love. It is
done through prayer communication.

"And now these three remain: faith, hope
and love. But the greatest of these is love."
Corinthians 13:13

This most important closeness is not learned
by education but by experience in prayer. It
is a fellowship of personalities, meaning the
Divine and man. People were made to live
by guidance in relationship, never alone on
their own.

"The beginning of wisdom is this: Wisdom
is supreme. Therefore get wisdom.
Though it cost all you have, whatever else
you get, get understanding.
Cherish her, and she will exalt you;
embrace her, and she will honor you.
She will give you a garland to grace your
head
and present you with a glorious crown."
Listen, my son, accept what I say,

and the years of your life will be many.
I instruct you in the way of wisdom
and lead you along straight paths. When you
walk, your steps will not be hampered;
when you run, you will not stumble.
Hold on to instruction, do not let it go;
guard it well, for it is your life."
Proverbs 4:7-13

Depression

Do you feel someone or something sucking
the life energy out of your life? Is a big hole
in your middle leaving you feeling sad and
little interest in doing anything? People with
depression feel sad, hopeless for many days
on end. It is hard to get going, even dressing,
or eating a meal. It is hard to sleep. There is
little energy and sometimes a continuous
desire for suicide and death because there is
no hope it will ever end.

There are medications and psychological
help which can help over time. The issue is
energy vampires or energy sucking demons
who have found a way to make a death hold

grip on the soul of a person. There are people whose very presence drains the energy of those around them. They can be attractive, verbose, and ostentatious. They are visible representations of the hidden demons working through people or directly attaching to souls.

Medical science does not know the cause as with most mind issues. The main cause from a faith perspective is a breakdown in communication with the Divine. When people seek their own will they open themselves up to life energy sucking entities that prey on extremely self-willed people. When people get into this situation it is going to take continuous prayer in Jesus Name, by His Blood Sacrifice, and the Divine Will to be done always. A whole new commitment to the Divine to love Him more than anything or anyone needs to be done.

Thinking

Are you a thinking person? The process of thinking begins with a question. The mind then stirs to action to reveal from the question that you are and what information is available. Thinking does not attract what you want to yourself, but it reveals to a person their soul which itself attracts what their soul wants to a person.

"for as he thinks within himself, so he is." Proverbs 23:7

"Men do not attract what they WANT, but what they ARE." Charles Allen's book 1903.

How can people who want to change their life change their soul, what they are? The first century church knew the answer to this question. They asked Jesus to change them and He did. It is the same today. Is this even possible to change the person we are? With prayer and the Divine it is still possible today.

Over and over again the quantum world is

revealing that determinism is not the final say. Cause and effect are only part of the story. A person's mind has a part in the outcome. Was Jesus right when He said that by Faith mountains can be moved, or trees uprooted and thrown into the sea? When is He ever wrong?

If people want a better life the answer seems to be to change their soul. For what a person's soul is this is also what their life is. Life just responds to form whatever their soul calls into being or action. Your life is who you are and who you are is your life. People cannot hide from themselves. Life truly reveals it to them.

What about good and evil influence? Evil is always around to help people degrade their soul which will in turn degrade their life. Good is always around, for a while, to help people upgrade their soul which will in turn upgrade their life. Once again witness the enormous power of choice to form our soul which determines our life even more than cause and effect according to quanta theory.

Jealousy

No power on earth can placate or satisfy a jealous man. His fury is like a volcano whose eruption can only be safely avoided, never confronted. When his pride is insulted past the point of apology, it is too late. Scatter to the wind. He is by nature beyond control at this point. Sanity has flown out the window. By reason of insanity there are no limits to his revenge. Do not push people too far. Killing the body is one thing. Killing self-image leads to revenge beyond any limits. Scripture warns about insults. We should listen.

Is the Divine jealous? Very much so. Why would the fury of God be ignited like a jealous man? Made in His image a man responds like the Divine. Once the Holy One has entered into a contract of person to person by way of His Son Jesus, the fury of the Divine is kindled to no satisfaction when a person reneges on the deal made. It is so insulting.

"For the LORD your God is a consuming fire, a jealous God." Deuteronomy 4:24

"How much more severely do you think someone deserves to be punished who has trampled the Son of God underfoot, who has treated as an unholy thing the blood of the covenant that sanctified them, and who has insulted the Spirit of grace?" Hebrews 10:29

"It is a terrifying thing to fall into the hands of the living God." Hebrews 10:31

Will these scripture warnings stop people whose self-image has been too deeply insulted? Nothing and no one can stop them. The safe thing is to not let it go this far. Watch out for insults and defuse them before the fuse gets ignited.

Hiding

Why do the wealthy hide behind gates, security, fences, islands, mansions, and generally unrecognizable? There are many reasons. It depends on the person and their circumstances. But generally, they want privacy because everyone wants what they have. Their real friends are few. Most acquaintances cannot be trusted. It's lonely at the top.

This is not fault finding. It is as it should be in this world. More importantly let's talk about the Divine. His wealth is beyond any measurement. Wealth is not important to Him, only that it is used efficiently. What is important to Him? Would you believe friendship? He respects and wants respect. He is not going to change Who He Is. So, friends have to learn to respect Him as He Is.

The Divine is a Gambler. He played a big hand and lost. But, He knew He would lose only to ultimately win. He came to earth as the Son to stay in the game for real friends. He hides His wealth and won real friends. Without showing His material wealth He shows Himself to people personally and individually on an intuitive experience level. It is a personal friendship deal of respect for respect both ways. Those people who accept

Him on a personal level He adopts into His family. Every future need is supplied. Wealthy people already know their friends are few, but it is worth it to them.

To qualify, it has to be a personal experience with complete personal trust. The saddest news in the world is the person who is contacted for Divine friendship and refuses for selfish reasons. Many people lacking wealth respond with acceptance. They don't have any pride, or material things to lose. Their soul is as valuable as anyone's. Whatever little they have they wisely count it as nothing and gain everything. The Divine wins real friends without showing His wealth. Poor people win the Best Friend they will ever have. Wealthy people understand wealth like few others. They need to at least reason it out to consider responding with a yes the next time the Spirit makes one more contact offering of Divine Friendship. Otherwise, consider the advice of Jesus who said this astonishing thing to the wealthy, "I tell you, use worldly wealth to gain friends for yourselves, so that when it is gone, you will be welcomed into eternal dwellings." Luke 16:9

Epiphany

Have you had a sudden intuitive experience into reality? This may be the personal experience with the Divine. It is way beyond intellect which is supportive but never enough. This personal experience is what people need and accept or reject. It changes people. In religious terms it is a calling. Often it happens during some religious event such as reading scripture, hearing scripture in a sermon, or baptism. Some epiphanies are stronger than others. They continue throughout a person's life once they begin if the initiate accepts them. Blaise Pascal, born 1623, is a famed intellect, scientist who experienced the presence of the Divine reading John 17. It was far beyond intellect. He famously said, "The heart has its reasons that reason knows not of." This is a person's moment in time, their proof. It is a new birth, a born again experience. If a person really wants to know, are emotionally open to the truth, the leap of faith can occur. It is as Jesus said when a person hears Him knocking on the door and opens to Him. Treasure your epiphany(s). It may be all you get. The Apostle Paul had many. Doubting Thomas finally had one that overwhelmed him. The risen Jesus invited him to put his hand into His side and the holes in His hands. Thomas believed after that. Not everyone is given an epiphany like that, but whatever comes is life changing and never forgotten. This is a person's calling, their moment when the Divine reaches out to them and makes personal contact with them. It is meant to be the start of a new relationship. Yes, it is a kind of human marriage which the fortunate experience an in love event and both humans know they are meant to be. They are soulmates. Too many marriages are only contractual business arrangements based on some practical attraction. Cupid is still around. Marriage to Jesus however is a heartfelt epiphany, beyond intellectual proof like a soulmate discovery moment. Say yes, for the moment may never come again as people who have heard their calling found out. When Jesus is knocking on the door of your heart open it for the wonder of a new life of proof and fulfillment.

Circle

What goes around comes around? Is this really true? More ways than people may know. The very basis of Jesus Kingdom on earth now is this cause and effect principle. Give and receive ... receive and give, not keep it all. Learning the hard way, even nations are still learning to share on a fair basis. The heart of romance is the circle. Bonding occurs by sharing the great energy that comes into a sharing relationship. Robbers not only keep what is theirs but take what is others without permission. The idea is to keep and take from others but not share because there will be less for me. This is why it is hard to believe that reality is based in reciprocity. We help others and others help us.

Around and around it goes. What makes this circle work? The Divine. It is always the Divine. Somehow, someway, the Holy One has unlimited resources. He is the Master. When people share love, kindness, help from Him, and then He sees to it that others share back the same or more. Even bad things come back around. The Divine makes sure goes around comes around. It is the basis of His society. Jesus said in effect that people who share will be given more to share. The Divine is the storehouse that never runs out. This is why it works. The Lord is the Source. Give, He says, and you will receive good measure, pressed down, shaken together, running over, and poured into your lap. Does this work with money? Sometimes and sometimes not. It depends on the reason. Most, if not all things depend on the reason. The basis of satan's kingdom on earth is self only. The basis of the Divine's Kingdom on earth is sharing. The Supplier has unlimited supplies to fund any member of His family. The Circle is Divine and always will be.

Roleplay

Would you marry someone who only plays a set of behaviors? Of course not. Why? Simply because they are playing and not being themselves. Consciously or unconsciously people assume behaviors, not their own, acting a part. Husbands, wives, doctors, nurses, business leaders, and many more may act out their society impressionist roles. It is a lie, intentional or not. People do this because they want approval though they are not ready for the specific behavior. They pretend to be something they are not.

Maybe this is what Socrates was talking about in saying, "know thyself"? Others say, "to thy own self be true". People can use role play in a positive way to learn about the role, but who wants to marry someone who is never themselves. That seems ugly even on the face of it. What a ruse! It is guaranteed to destroy marriages, families, and even yourself. Was this not Judas Iscariot's issue in pretending to follow Jesus and then betray Him?

In dating people often play a role, put their best step forward, and long as possible never reveal who they are. People get hurt so bad. Trusting a person to be someone they are not eventually comes crashing down. Good admonition is to remember the people who matter to you are those who do not mind what you say and do. They love you anyway. People who should not matter to you are those who mind what you say and do because you do not do and say by the role they expect of you. They are not true friends. Do not play a role. Be the role, not falsely assume it, and a person will naturally have the right friends and enemies. Be a follower of Jesus, not a Judas, a pretender, or fence straddle.

Role playing is good for actors in movies, learning, and psychotherapy, but never all the time to hide the truth, hide from the truth, and never are true. Simple as it may seem, Hiding is not necessary. In fact, it is counterproductive and in the end destructive. Be real. These are the only people who have a shot at being happy. This is not promoting a libertine life. Respect, manners, etiquette may be whitewash on a hog, but at least the hog is cute enough to be palatable and to serve as a bad example. How sad to live a life and never know who you are, never find the Divine, and have only pretentious friends. Only a real life has any meaning. Love, romance, relationships are based on true, real, not pretense. Who wants a stranger for a mate or friend? Certainly the Divine does not. Relationships are too intimate for role playing.

Torture

Using severe physical or mind pain on a person to punish, to make do, to say, or for pleasure of the giver is torture. Its severity and motivation gives it various names. Such names would be discipline, enhanced interrogation, or sadism. The Divine is a loving ole guy who would never torture? Thinking this means people do not know Him. First, He is not old. He has been around longer than dirt. He is young and never changes. The passage of time does not age Him.

As a Heavenly Parent the Divine does discipline because He loves His people. Discipline is part of maturity in any endeavor. It takes much skill to discipline, not too much, not too little, and with the proper motivation. Parents who hate their children let them run wild. Those who love them make rules and regularly enforce them. Scripture warns parents not to overdo it and break their heart. History, written right or wrong, including scripture is a record of spiritual discipline of the Divine or satan upon people. The Divine has the last word, but satan has much of a free reign by choice until his time is up. Both want the souls of people. Each uses discipline with varying degrees of severity but with different motivation.

Romans 11:22 "Behold then the kindness and severity of God; to those who fell, severity, but to you, God's kindness, if you continue in His kindness; otherwise you also will be cut off."

The pivotal act is faith. Keep faith and

kindness continues. Reject faith and severity happens. Both the Divine and satan are deal makers. The Divine offers unlimited personality health, love, good relationships forever by faith agreement. Then satan offers varying amounts of materialism, wealth, power, knowledge and pleasure in this world. Each will use different amounts of discipline to regulate the deal. People should not try them in a fickle manner. Each is far more powerful than people know. Make a good deal and stick with it.

Vision

Is it important to have a goal? It may seem easier to work on the steps to get there though people may not know where they are going. Sometimes grocery shopping can work this way. The trip around the store seeing things on the shelf reminds of what we need. This is not very efficient in the long run and we may just buy things we do not need as much. It is always best to know where we are going, what we need to accomplish to have what we need and therefore how to get there. To put it simply, humans need to know what they are going to do first before they figure out how to do it. Otherwise it is the blind leading the blind. Jesus said they both fall into the ditch. Christians always need a vision for the Church in each generation. Christians need to know for what to pray. Then the steps of action to get there will appear also. For the people of the Divine it is first revelation or vision, and then follows the steps. This is so true in business, family, marriage, where to live, interpersonal relations, and other important stages of life. First computer programmers figure out what they want the computer to do. Second, they then figure out the steps the computer needs to follow to get it done. It is always the horse, then the cart. Does the Divine have anything to do with happy human life? Very much so. He reveals first the goal, and then the steps.

Proverbs 29:18, "If people can't see what the Divine is doing, they stumble all over themselves; but when they attend to what He reveals, they are most blessed."

John 15:5 said Jesus, "I am the vine; you are the branches. If you remain in me and I in you, you will bear much fruit; apart from me you can do nothing."

The Divine is all about love. It starts with a prayer life so a person can have visions. This means a person's business products need to be all about respect for the feelings of others. A good marriage should be chosen so a happy family can follow. A happy family results in seeded generations that follow. A happy Church life for good interactions will be revealed. Is any or all of this possible in today's world? Very much so. It starts with Divine visions given to people who pray. People need to know where they are going before they can figure out how to get there. Yes, it is simple to say, and also simple to do, if people have a patient prayer life.

Etiquette

You know it. This is polite, customary,

behavior in our society, group, and business. It is protocol, usually unwritten rules of accepted behavior, good form, decorum, that may reflect a person's status. The purpose is to show respect for yourself, and others feelings first because it is not all about you. It has even been suggested that manners at the dinner table helped reduce violence in the street (Pinker). We may have overlooked that Jesus taught etiquette as a form of humility. Good strokes for good folks is probably a saying. Strokes bring out love and respect for the occasion. Courtly behavior comes from the teaching given to Knights on how to behave in the presence of the King.

Luke 14:10 Said Jesus, "But when you are invited, take the lowest place, so that when your host comes, he will say to you, 'Friend, move up to a better place.' Then you will be honored in the presence of all the other guests." or

Luke 7:41-47 Said Jesus, "Two people owed money to a certain moneylender. One owed him five hundred denarii and the other fifty.

Neither of them had the money to pay him back, so he forgave the debts of both. Now which of them will love him more?"

Simon replied, "I suppose the one who had the bigger debt forgiven."

"You have judged correctly," Jesus said.

Then he turned toward the woman and said to Simon, "Do you see this woman? I came into your house. You did not give me any water for my feet, but she wet my feet with her tears and wiped them with her hair. You did not give me a kiss, but this woman, from the time I entered, has not stopped kissing my feet. You did not put oil on my head, but she has poured perfume on my feet. Therefore, I tell you, her many sins have been forgiven—as her great love has shown. But whoever has been forgiven little loves little."

Perhaps etiquette shows more than respect for the feelings of people in front of us. It may show our respect for the Divine above us? Should people in a world like this show etiquette? Behavior in this world is not only about this world. There are angels and the Divine present also who constantly watch.

Identity

In this world can someone steal your identity? Not really. They can apprehend a person's information that is private and personal. But no one can be you. Each person is unique, one of a kind, in the whole universe. There is only one and one only of you. A person does not have to be someone else. Each human being is special. The question for many people is how then can I fully be me? Life on this planet takes air, sunlight, water, and food to keep the body alive. There are no two like bodies. Yes, true. Even identical twins with the same DNA are still different, as for example identical twins have not the same fingerprints. How the baby hand of one twin touches the amniotic sac affects their fingerprint. But what of the personality, the most unique feature of a person? Nature gives a person their DNA, but Nurture or environment like sleep, food, gives them their specialness.

To be fully who we are people need interaction with the Spirit of the Divine. Many people would like to be who they are and all they can be. This is why bullying in schools is so harmful. High Schoolers cannot escape their social environment and choose to commit suicide perhaps to protect their uniqueness. However we look at it. People are one of a kind. They do not have to be someone else, who they are not. Not even two stars in the universe are the same. The Creator knows each of His stars by name. Did not Jesus say that each person is so unique that the numbers of hairs are known to the Creator? Jesus went on to imply that the special identity of a person is such that they should not even try to change it as it cannot be done. With artificial intelligence, cyborg or machine parts, crisper genetic manipulation are on the horizon. It may be okay to enhance or improve human nature, but should humans ever try to change the uniqueness? We are going see what happens and find out.

Evil spirits are a spiritual cancer on the personality of a person. They are abusive, degrading, and coercive to the identity. Jesus hated them. He would not allow them even to speak to Him. They were terrified of Him and begged for mercy. He removed thousands of them from the lives of people. The scripture does not exaggerate when it says it is a terrifying thing to fall into the hands of the Living God. Jesus further advised people to never insult, abuse a child whose angel beholds the face of the Divine. Abusers would be doing themselves a favor if they tied a large stone to their neck and drowned themselves in the sea. From conception people have a unique identity. No two snowflakes are the same. Each is unique. It is reported at the atomic level the number of possible pattern arrangements of the snowflake molecule is many times greater than the entire number of atoms in the universe. The identity of a human is special like no other or ever will be. Maybe people should love themselves more?

Profiling

It is all spiritual. It is mysterious, meaning difficult to understand, puzzling, identify, and so on. When the Spirit is added, life happens, harmony occurs, and well-being results. The opposite result is when the Spirit withdraws or pulls away some. The Church of Jesus experienced the addition of the Holy Spirit like never before since Eden. Profiling or fear and suspicion were erased for the Church by this event. Profiling is inherent in the nature of people until they are born again by the Spirit. Life, health, harmony between people and within people is again all spiritual. How much Spirit and how little Spirit is the defining measure of it all. So, how can humans have more Spirit? They can ask, give thanks, and share. Fulfillment in life is what humans do with their gifts. How much they have to share is decided by the Spirit. What people do with what they have is fulfillment. Jesus implied that those who have and share will be given more to share. Those who have and do not share will see what they have taken away and given to those who do share. The Divine is also in business for profit. However, what is valuable to Him is far more than money. The greatest value is interpersonal relations. Credit there is highly valued.

Dying

People know that human life is terminal. "The Lord gives and the Lord takes away," said Job 1:21. Death and suffering is not dignified. It is the consequence of undignified behavior. Do people have any rights at all? Do they have the right to end their suffering when their life is terminal? Medicine eases pain. Medicine eases debilitating pain. Jesus cured the sick, even raised the dead. The Divine has promised a general resurrection, some to inclusion and some to exclusion. People often have one opinion before they walk in another's shoes and a second different opinion when they go through a similar experience. Is pain the Will of the Divine? It is certainly a consequence of contrary behavior, and the result of the pain of martyrdom. In this last case people choose loyalty to the Divine with the pain of death. They choose to end their life for His cause and are justified by their faith and love. See Hebrews 11. People probably cannot answer this question of choosing to die with dignity when suffering a terminal illness until they need too. Anymore, it is always a brave new world.

Morality / Immorality

Both of these behaviors, one proper and one improper, are best understood side by side. The intentions, decision, actions will make one behavior moral and another immoral. The motivation maybe fun, revenge, achievement, respect, or approval. The behavior of the followers of the Divine and the archenemy satan would be moral versus immoral according to their view.

People have strong feelings about what is moral. From people to people, culture to culture, what is moral can be different. Yet, because of common set of human emotions there are basic principles of what is moral and immoral. Proper behavior can relate to the society or world in which we live, or according to our faith in a personal Creator, and perhaps both. Conscience informs us of our behavior as moral or not based upon our accepted definition of morality.

It gets complicated for sure. Conscience is important for health, and well-being. For Christians the point is that humans can never behave properly to satisfy the Nature of the Divine. To join His Society a new birth is required by means of a spiritual baptism.